SEEK

WORKBOOK FOR CAREER

KNOW &

AND PERSONAL DEVELOPMENT

PLAN

Naviane Collier

TABLE OF CONTENTS

ACKNOWLEDGMENT

*To my husband, Gabe: Thank you for inspiring
and encouraging me through this writing process.*

*Thank you, Lord, for your power
and wisdom through this journey.*

INTRODUCTION

———

HELLO, MY NAME IS NAVIANE AND I AM A LIFE COACH. I KNOW YOU may be wondering why did she introduce herself like that. Well, for a very long time I considered myself a failure even with a Master's Degree. I went from one job to another hoping to find my purpose. It took me falling on my face praying, ask God to reveal my purpose to me. He did just that, once I found my way back to Him and myself. Now I want to help you find your purpose.

When asked as a child, "What do you want to be when you grow you," that question was one of the most stress-free questions you could have asked me. I wanted to be a psychologist; I always knew I desired to help people. My question to you is whether you would give the same response now or did you stop dreaming because life has hit you.

Imagine with me for a second, you are standing in front of what I will call the Wall of Opportunities. On the Wall of Opportunities are different careers, choices, purposes, and paths; you're able to grab one and put yourself into that profession. So, you choose one without paying much attention to the occupation, then poof: you become a lawyer. Working in that field, it has become depressing because of the long hours of studying for cases, so poof: you are back in front of the wall. At this time, are you going to just grab another one without thinking, or are you going to take your time before picking one?

Maybe some of you would snatch another career without thinking because the potential of coming back to the wall to grab another career seems endless. For the group who would take their time in selecting the next career choice and be more deliberate: this interactive workbook is for you. Actually, this workbook will help both types of career hunters make a wise career decision. This book will help you write out your goals, challenge your way of thinking, ask you difficult questions to meditate on, and help you organize your life through varies activities. So, let's get started: first seeking, next knowing, then planning.

PART ONE

Who are you?

DURING OUR TIME HERE ON EARTH, WE CHANGE JUST LIKE THE seasons. You are not the same person reading this book today as you were ten years ago. I know for a fact that I am not the same person I was ten years ago, or even five years ago. In my twenties I was scared, angry with life, unforgiving, rude, and disrespectful. I listened to others' thoughts about me and did not stand up for myself. I made poor decisions and changed a lot about myself to please those around me. As the years rolled by, and I found a deep relationship with God and myself, I began to change for the better. I can honestly say that I am happy being myself, I would not change that for the world. We all need the opportunity to get to know ourselves again. Please allow me the opportunity to help you reintroduce you to yourself.

Answer the following questions using complete sentences:

How old are you?

Are you currently in school or taking classes? If not, would you like to go back to school?

Do you have children? If so, how many?

Are you currently employed? If so, what is your occupation?

Do you attend church? If so, what is the name of the church?

List your greatest talents or attributes?

Describe a time when your talents or gifts brought you joy.

List five things you like about yourself and why you like each item?

1.)

2.)

3.)

4.)

5.)

List five things you would like to change about yourself and why you want to change each thing?

1.)

2.)

3.)

4.)

5.)

What are the four things you want people to say about you after you leave the room?

1.)

2.)

3.)

4.)

Do you believe people are saying those things now? Why or why not?

Contrast the person you are in private, along with who you are in public. Why do you think these differences exist?

How much time do you commit to each of the following people or activity in any average day:

Family and friends _____

Yourself _____

Work/Career _____

School _____

Social media _____

Watch television _____

Personal goals _____

Housework _____

Now, rank these items 1 through 8 in importance to you, with 1 being the most important and 8 being the least.

Write out your thoughts about the list.

List three important personal values:

1.)

2.)

3.)

List three important accomplishments within the past five years?

1.)

2.)

3.)

What is your end all be all career goal and why?

Based on your answer to the previous question, do you have time to make your dreams become a reality? Why or why not?

Are you happy?

Looking in the mirror and honestly assessing yourself is very difficult. We live in a world where fitting into a role that others want us to be is typical. I will make the case that knowing who you are while living your best life and allowing people to genuinely love you for who you are, is more important.

PART TWO

What do you want?

FINDING YOUR PASSION IS VERY HARD. LIFE DOES NOT COME WITH A user's manual to help guide us through each turn. I challenge you to spend twenty minutes, listing out what makes you joyful and what also makes you gloomy. Knowing what makes you joyful will help you focus on the positive and which will help you not give energy to the negativity. Why not choose happiness!

This exercise should help you find your true purpose.

Joyful	Gloomy

How did you choose the things that make you joyful?

How did you choose the things that make you gloomy?

PART THREE

Why you?

MANY OF US CAN WRITE A WHOLE BOOK EXPLAINING WHY WE shouldn't pursue our dreams or pursue the career we truly desire. We tend to allow past setbacks and challenges overwhelm, then quash our dreams. We start questioning our abilities and personal nature and choose to alter pursuing our desires. I use to kill my dreams before anyone else had a chance. But, I challenged myself to write out the reasons I deserved the career I wanted, the marriage I wanted, and the life I always imagined. Now, I am challenging you to do the same thing. I have a quick exercise for you to complete that's called the Seven Whys.

You'll need a serious partner for this part. I want you and your partner to perform the "Seven Levels Deep Exercise." I got this practice from *The Millionaire Success Habits*, a book written by Dean, G. (2016). It is a wonderful book. This exercise is also available online at http://www.7levelsdeep.com. Begin by having your partner ask you: "What do you truly want to do with your life?" Then, they should proceed to ask you "why" seven times. Please respond by answering the questions using complete sentences each time. The person answering needs to respond each time. This exercise can elicit some strong emotions. Write down your response to the last "why" and how you felt during the exercise. If you don't have a partner with whom to practice the exercise, use the listed website as a guide.

Write your response to the Seven Whys?

Describe how you felt during the Seven Whys exercise?

After completing the why exercise, write out why you desire your dreams.

Write out why you deserve the things you desire for your life. Take your time and think of as many reasons as possible.

PART FOUR

What have the naysayers said?

I WILL NEVER FORGET TELLING MY FAMILY THAT I WANTED TO BECOME a psychologist. I did not expect their response, which was, "Why would you want to work with crazy people? You need to think of something else to do." I didn't understand why their response wounded me so badly then, but now I do. Like many people, I had opened my heart to my family, friends, coworkers, educators, and church members. When they belittled my dreams, it cut deeply and left scars. We let the people in our inner circle of trust know our sincere desires and when one of those individuals disregard our dreams, it hurts. Maybe they don't understand your dream. Maybe they're envious, negative, intimidated, or inexperienced with what you have presented to them.

Have you ever told someone your dreams and had them respond negatively?

What did the person say?

How did those words make you feel?

Remember, anytime you begin to work on yourself and go for what you want, people will begin to tell you that you shouldn't. Here's what you need to do: write down what you anticipate they will say, then write down your comeback response.

"I can do all things through Christ that strengthen you."

Philippians 4:13, NKJV
Scripture taken from the New King James Version

Criticism	Response

PART FIVE

What are you afraid of?

I WAS LISTENING TO AN ERIC THOMAS'S (ET) MOTIVATIONAL VIDEO, and he asked, "What are you afraid of?" That statement really disturbed me; I couldn't stop thinking about the question. So, I grabbed a sheet of paper and wrote down my fears. While I was writing, tears began to flow down my face onto my sheet of paper. I realized for the first time that I was living in fear and not in faith. I always believed I was a person of faith, a true go-getter until I saw that video. Then ET stated, "Now, write down what you would have possibly accomplished if you weren't living in fear."

Here is the chance to write your list of fears and accomplishment. Be one hundred percent honest with yourself.

Fears	Accomplishments

Do not live in fear. Embrace freedom and believe.

PART SIX

Change lanes and decide.

ONE OF MY BIGGEST PET PEEVES IS DRIVING BEHIND SOMEONE GOING slower than the speed limit. That frustrates me to the core, and I always think: "Just speed up, please!" But, whenever that happens to me, I have two options: I can stay behind the slow driver and remain upset, or I change lanes and hope for the best. We have those same options in life. We can remain in fear and never soar, or take the risk, jump, and position ourselves to soar. Which option are you going to choose? You have already worked through:

- Who you are.
- What you want.
- Why you.
- What the naysayers will say.
- What you fear.

The ball is in your court. Are you going to change lanes and make the decision to soar, or are you going to remain behind the slow car?

Stay behind: If you choose to stay behind the slow car, write down why. Is this due to fear?

Change lanes: How did you feel making this decision to soar?

PART SEVEN

Create a purpose board.

"Where there is no vision, the people perish."

Proverbs 29:18, KJV

IN THIS SECTION, I WILL GUIDE YOU THROUGH CREATING A PURPOSE board or vision board. I use the term "purpose board" because we each have a purpose here on earth, and our goal should be to fulfill that purpose. You have done the exercises to establish who you are and the Seven Whys. You have identified your passions, which will be further explored using the purpose board to sort out your desires, goals, and dreams. Many people like to put together their purpose board at the beginning of the new year. Keep in mind God does not just call people at the beginning of the year. Your vision can come to you whenever; you just have to be listening. Let's get started!

To create a purpose board, gather these important items:

- A dose of creativity
- Magazines (as many as you feel you need)
- One cardboard
- Glue stick or double-sided tape (your preference)
- A pair of scissors

Follow these instructions:

Step one: Go through the magazines and select the images that inspire your purpose.

Step two: Cut out everything necessary to get your purpose out of your heart and onto that board.

Step three: Once you have the images that motive you then arrangement them on your cardboard (this is the time to get creative). You could also do your board in categories or you could just do it in a way that feels visually inspirational to you.

Step four: Once you're settled securely with an arrangement that influences you, secure the images with the glue or double-sided tape.

Congratulation! You have now completed your purpose board. I like to take a picture of my board and use it as the screen saver on my computer and cellphone. It is always with me, reminding me to push through adversity and work hard. Send photos of your purpose board to my Instagram at @navi_j2s. Can't wait to see what you put together. No worries, I share my board on my Instagram page check it out.

PART EIGHT

Create a routine.

I CAN RECALL GROWING UP WITH A STRICT ROUTINE EVERY MORNING. We all had a set time that we needed to be up in the morning, to get in the shower, then out the door for school. Now, for many of us we haven't had a routine since we were children. Routines provide children with stability and order, which for many adults would say they need stability and order; a daily routine can provide that. By planning out your day you can prepare for obstacles big and small. Having a routine can also help you evaluate your progress for your goals, work, and personal needs.

Consider this, just by going with the flow each day can only take you but so far, you need to put a plan in place every day. When starting a routine, you need will power, discipline, and motivation. Sticking with a daily routine can be difficult at times because life can be unpredictable and that's where that will power, and discipline should kick in.

How many times have you been stressed, anxious, or even overwhelmed about how your day is going? You can reduce anxiety and increase control with a simple routine or creating a to do list. Never start your day without a goal, a list, or a plan for the day. Evan Carmichael on his YouTube channel called BelieveLife, talks about many famous people who live by a daily routine. Check it out. I provided you with a template of what my to-do list looks like. I put things in order of most important to least important. You can use the one I presented you or you can create your own.

Routine Tracker Guide

	Most Important	Least Important
Monday		
Tuesday		
Wednesday		
Thursday		
Friday		
Saturday		
Sunday		

Get a planner and track your day, watch the amount of time you will gain in your life with a simple routine.

PART NINE

Stop procrastinating.

HAVE YOU EVER SAID ONE OF THESE FAMOUS STATEMENTS:

"I just don't feel like doing this today."

"I will get that done tomorrow."

"I forgot about that."

We spend more time showering than we do on achieving our goals! We all have responsibilities and things we want to accomplish, but we find ourselves pushing our goals off day after day. We become unmotivated, careless, or become afraid of failure. We are not born procrastinators; we become procrastinators for many reasons: the feeling of revolting, a kick of adrenaline for doing things at the last minute, fear of failure, or fear of making the wrong decision.

I would procrastinate out of fear of other people's opinions of me and my ability to do a job well. I was born to inspire and motivate others. Let me help you stop being a procrastinator with these quick tips and tricks to align your effort with your purpose and make your dreams a reality.

- Limit distraction;
- Put the phone down and turn off your notification;
- Break tasks into small pieces;
- Make a to do list, and work on the hardest task first;
- Surround yourself with people who have drive and discipline;
- Start for fifteen minutes, then push yourself to work on a task longer; and
- Watch a motivational video before starting a task.

Stop putting off your dreams. Don't settle for a lifetime of unfulfilled possibilities. Make a promise today that you'll stop making excuses. Push for what you want.

Name: _____

Date: _____

Promise yourself by signing and dating this vow here.

PART TEN

Find a place to create.

FOR A WHILE, I THOUGHT I COULD TAKE CARE OF MY PROFESSIONAL tasks in the same office day after day. What began to happen was I would associate my home office with work only, which made me dread entering into that room. You may have heard the expression, "A clean space equals a clean mind," which is true. I like the saying, "a creative space equals triumph." Find one or several locations where you feel creative. You may have to create a creative space by adding elements that evolves the feeling of freedom and happiness.

I needed several locations to be my mental sanctuary because I found myself becoming disengaged using the same workspace. You may need to declutter your creative space. In most cases, having papers, snacks, cups, etc. on your desk can make you feel overwhelmed and stressed; these elements in your workspace can lead to procrastination. I want you to remain motivated, disciplined, and excited about going after your desires. In order to remain that way, you need to find a place that will help you to become creative and productive. Using the following pictures as a guide.

A　　　　　　　　　　　　**B**

Which workspace do you find more creative and productive? A or B?

Remember, we must find, clean, create, and soar!

PART ELEVEN

Put your phone down.

FOR MANY OF US, OUR PHONES ARE OUR LIFELINES, WE USUALLY don't leave home without them. If we happen to I'm sure most of us would turn around and get it. Some of us wake up in the morning, and the first thing we do is grab for our phones. Instead of giving thanks for the day, we just hop on social media and begin scrolling. I'm not sure when we became so dependent on this pocket size technology. I want to propose a challenge for you, avoid checking your phone during the first hour of the day and the last hour before you go to bed. This will allow your mind time to charge in order to take on the day and rest before bed.

I want to tell you a story: one day I got up early and grabbed my phone as I was waking up. I checked my Instagram, Facebook, and Snapchat and watched some YouTube videos. I checked my emails, and when I looked at the clock, it was 12:30 in the afternoon. Three and a half hours had passed. I could not believe how much time I wasted. Many of you are wasting time watching other people's false realities. We all wish for more time in the day. If you put your phone away and focus, you will have more time to work toward your goals. If your phone is not making you money, put it down. How much time do you spend a day on social media platforms? Be honest with yourself. Be the real you, not the pretend you. Use the following activity to record how much time you spend on each social media platform.

Record your time here:

Twitter	
Facebook	
YouTube	
Snapchat	
Instagram	

What can you get done with the time you spend on social media? Let's begin with creating a schedule for social media use. Use the chart to schedule how long and what days to use each platform.

Platform	Time Spent	Day of the Week
Twitter		
Facebook		
YouTube		
Snapchat		
Instagram		

Now list the other things you can accomplish with the rest of the hours of a day. Schedule success in your day.

PART TWELVE

Who's in your circle?

"Show me your friends,
and I'll tell you who you are."

proverb

THE MOST INFLUENTIAL PEOPLE IN YOUR LIFE ARE THE FIVE PEOPLE closest to you. This is why being very intentional about having the right inner circle is extremely important. You can tell if you have the right people in your life because they will challenge you to be better, they're honest with you, likewise you with them. They'll be there during difficult times, helping you to learn new things and help you develop qualities to improve yourself. Friends can also include parents, spouse, and siblings. When fostering new growth, it may require you to expand your horizons.

Here's a list to use when looking for new friends:

- Do they share your same values, integrity, and beliefs?
- Can you trust and look up to them?
- Will they stay with you during the highs and lows in life?
- Do they push you to do better each day?
- Are they passionate, driven, and insightful?
- Do they care about people and animals?
- Do they have a proven track record of being loyal?
- Can they teach you a thing or two?

Who are your five closest friends?

1.)

2.)

3.)

4.)

5.)

Why did you choose them as friends?

1.)

2.)

3.)

4.)

5.)

What are they adding to your life?

1.)

2.)

3.)

4.)

5.)

Do you think it is time for you to get new friends? Why
or why not?

Describe a typical conversation with your friends.

Are you afraid of leaving your friends behind and
going for what you want?

Would you be afraid what others will say if you decide
to put your dreams first?

Your Friends vs You

If we truly want to grow and become better, we have to check ourselves and the friends we hang around.

Have you ever judged someone for a facial expression?

Have you ever judged someone for their body language?

Have you ever judged someone for the way they speak?

Have you ever judged someone for their personal appearance?

If you answered yes to any of the questions, why do you think you judged others in these various situations?

Do you feel like you attract friends who are like you? If so, how do you think you can change that?

If you really want to know what people think about you, ask them. Remember that their response will be a mixture of truth and opinions.

PART THIRTEEN

Find a mentor.

IN PART TWELVE, I ASKED ABOUT WHO IS IN YOUR FRIENDSHIP CIRCLE.
Now, I want to draw your attention to the importance of mentorship. A lot of successful individuals will tell you that they had a great mentor who helped them become successful in their careers. Mentoring is important because of the knowledge a person can gain from a mentor. A mentor can teach you tips and tricks in their areas of expertise. I encourage you to find a mentor and get connected to new possibilities, resources, and people. You can also have an unofficial mentor that you have never met before. For instance, I have never met Michael Todd, but I feel like he has taught me about being true to myself.

Here are some benefits of having a mentor:

- They help you figure out the steps and plan for your journey.
- They will hold you accountable for achieving goals you set for yourself.
- They can help you with connection, knowledge, and routine to help you succeed.
- They may become a lifetime friend or teacher.

Consider this, the true goal of a mentor is to help you so that you can eventually help someone else. Think beyond your time here on earth, and be a blessing to someone else.

Do you currently have a mentor?

Do you feel like you need a mentor? Why or why not?

How would you want your mentor to help you?

PART FOURTEEN

Faith and works.

"Thus also faith by itself, if it does not have works, is dead."

James 2:17 (NKJV)
Scripture taken from the New King James Version

PEOPLE OFTEN QUESTION WHETHER IMPOSSIBLE THINGS WILL happen if we just have faith in them happening. Yes, absolutely somethings can happen if you just have faith. But, the Bible also tells us that faith without works is dead, which means that we have to put effort into getting what we want. That's like putting together a goals list and not setting a time frame of when you want to achieve those goals. You know you want these things to happen, but you have not attempted to put any effort into making them happen.

By now you should have created your purpose board. Now, it's time to add realistic dates and actions items to your purpose board. You need to make it detailed enough to challenge and motivate you, but don't become overwhelmed, just take on one action item at a time. Take on an action one item at a time. I do this exact exercise and gain positive results over and over again. I had to put myself on a rigorous schedule to get this book done. I was not going to let another goal pass me by.

Here are a few tips to help you get started:

- Make your goals specific, measurable, attainable, relevant, and time based, that is, SMART. You can find examples online.

- What actions are essential to reaching your goals?

- List the challenges to achieving your goals and create a plan to combat those things.

- Follow through with each goal before beginning the next.

Do you find yourself praying for things to happen and not working towards your prayers?

How much do you want your goals to become a reality? Be honest with yourself. Circle the corresponding number to how bad you want to achieve that goal.

1   2   3   4   5   6   7   8   9   10

PART FIFTEEN

How the 80/20 rule works?

MAYBE YOU'VE HEARD OF THE 80/20 RULE, IF NOT I WILL PROVIDE YOU a brief illustration of the rule. The 80/20 rule has many different viewpoints and is one of the most helpful concepts for life. The rule 80/20 came from Pareto who stumbled upon the concept when observing his peapods. He recognized that 20% of the peapods in his garden contained 80% of the peas later he discovered the same pattern everywhere else.

My approach and view of the 80/20 rule is 80% of what happens in your life is influenced by you and you only, and 20% is influenced by people or things around you. Which brings me to my next theme victor vs victim mentality. The victim mentality focuses on outward stresses and a victor focuses on inward confidence.

The victim thinks 80% of life is influenced by others while the victor would know 80% is influenced by ourselves. You must remember you cannot blame anybody if you have not given eighty percent of your effort. Viewing life this way will help transform your mindset, particularly if you're someone who is always playing the victim role.

Here are a few signs if you have been playing the victim role;

- You don't trust people.
- You love comparing yourself to others.
- You are very critical.
- You hold onto grudges.
- You don't mind cutting people out of your life.
- You believe it's all about you.
- You blame others a lot.
- You want people to sympathize with you.

Remember, you have to fight for your dreams harder than anyone else. You have to work, grind, and push each day it's your life. The next two questions will uncover how you can interpret the 80/20 rule.

Are you the victim or the victor?

How will you use the 80/20 rule?

PART SIXTEEN

Time to learn and grow.

IF YOU ARE LEARNING, THEN YOU ARE GROWING. THAT STATEMENT still holds so much truth til this day. Make a promise to forever be a student, especially when you are teaching others. Be open to learning from anyone no matter their age, gender, race, or religion. The difficult part comes when no one is available to help teach you what you need to know. But, there are plethora of useful services and learning tools available for free on the internet. Consider this list of free sources of information for career help:

- Google
- YouTube
- Online webinars

Free Online webinars

Reading books and participating in local volunteer opportunities are also great sources of information and guidance. You should always be feeding your mind daily challenging yourself to learn a new skill. You must continue to learn and pick up new skills which in the long run will make you more marketable.

What is the highest level of education you need in the career you want to pursue?

List some books you can read for help in the career you want to pursue?

List some webinars or training you can attend for free:

Remember, you don't always have to pay for knowledge.

PART SEVENTEEN

Manage what you have.

I CAN STILL RECALL ONE OF THE MANY CONVERSATIONS I HAD WITH my husband about becoming a motivational speaker. I kept giving him excuses as to why I couldn't get started at that moment. My husband said, "When are you going to stop talking about it, and just do it?" Ultimately, there was no way of knowing, if that career was for me if I didn't at least try. Stop holding on to fear, and pursue what really makes you happy. You may fail, but you will have another chance to get back up and try again. Here are some famous excuses we use when we are fearful:

- I just need to save a little more money.

- Nobody will listen to me.

- I just don't have the time right now.

- I have to wait until my kids grow up.

- I don't know where to start.

Don't use excuses to stay in a victim mindset. Learn to manage what you have and go for what you want. Don't allow another second to go by without jumping into the career you really want. Keep hearing "no" until you get that "yes." It only takes one yes to unlock the door of opportunity and blessing. Who in your life seems to pursue their dreams or career goals with no fear? List three people who pursued their careers with no money and no college education and their occupations:

1.)

2.)

3.)

What did you learn from the people you listed? How can you use their stories to help you with your career?

PART EIGHTEEN

Create and use a network.

YOU MAY BE FAMILIAR WITH THE TRUISM STATEMENT, "IT'S NOT always what you know, but who you know." Whenever you are searching for a job, knowing someone on the inside is very helpful. But when you're just getting starting you may not have connections on the inside; that's where networking on social and attending networking events are helpful. Networking can be awkward and uncomfortable, especially when you are trying to spark a connection with a total stranger. Unfortunately, networking is essential if you expect to meet people who can help your business or put you in touch with the right people. The more you connect with others the more comfortable you will be.

Here are three ways to network:

- LinkedIn,

- Social or professional events, and

- Close contacts, within people you already know.

I would encourage you to look online for some networking events in your area. Make sure the events will help you with your goals in some form or fashion. Just remember, networking does not stop at the event. Keep in contact with those individuals. Also, networking is a two-way street. You have to show the other person that they need you as much as you need them.

Here are a few questions and ideas to start those conversations at networking event:

- How are you different from the competition?

- How can you solve a problem for your client?

- Who are your targeted clients?

- What services or products are you offering?

- Can you introduce me to the person I need to know?

- Do you have recommendations for me?

- Do you have any advice for someone at my level?

Take some time and brainstorm additional questions to help prepare for your next networking event. The more you network, the easier networking becomes and the more connections you will make. You can find more questions to help you network at http://www.alduncan.net/networking-questions.html.

PART NINETEEN

Create a portfolio.

A RESUME CAN ASSIST YOU WITH GETTING A FOOT IN THE DOOR, BUT IN this new era a business portfolio is a better way to go. Marketing yourself can be hard, so let your portfolio do the talking for you. Let me help you create a portfolio that will net results. Keep in mind, you can't get clients without a portfolio. Your portfolio will help you show samples of your work and what you have to offer. Portfolios also add visual impact by showcasing accomplishments, and provide potential clients with information that sell your skills and products for you.

There are two different types of portfolio: a business portfolio and a product portfolio. The first thing you need to figure out is what are you showcasing to the client business or products. Once you have established that, start brainstorming how you want to set up your portfolio.

Here are a few things you can have in your portfolio:

- Resume

- Cover letter

- Letters of recommendation

- Work samples and project summaries

- Licenses, certificates, and other records

- Copies of awards and honors

- Client evaluations

- Goals and plans

- Descriptions of project

The goal of the portfolio is to showcase you and your capabilities. So, whatever you think best represent you, your services, and products should be included. You can always look online for ideas and samples, also check out my website for tons of resources www.jump2soar.org.

How do you feel about putting together a portfolio?

How can you see it benefiting your career?

PART TWENTY

What's your price tag?

"And whatever you do, do it heartily, as to the Lord and not to men, knowing that from the Lord you will receive the reward of the inheritance; for you serve the Lord Christ."

Colossians 3:23-24, NKJV
Scripture taken from the New King James Version

WHEN WE DON'T KNOW "WHO'S" WE ARE, WE CAN'T JUDGE HOW much we are worth. You cannot sell a product to a client if you cannot sell it to yourself. You have to believe in your abilities and what you can bring to a client to gain that client. When you do not know what you are worth, others will begin to tell you what they think you are worth. When you set your worth others will have no choice but to believe that value. Stop settling for what you are given, and go after what you really want. First seek, next know, then plan, and manifest your vision. If you feel like you are worth a million dollars, then that's what you need to demand. Don't allow yourself to be low balled.

Please check out Michael Todd's series on YouTube called Planted Not Buried if you are truly ready to change your life for the better. His series opened my eyes to my true worth and once I knew who I was, and "Who's" I was, then I understood how much I was worth.

Do you know how much you are worth? If so, how much?

What can you bring to the table, and how much does it cost?

Do you believe in what you are offering or what you have?

PART TWENTY-ONE

Repeat this over and over.

"Death and life are in the power of the tongue."

Proverbs 18:21,N KJV
Scripture taken from the New King James Version

THE LAW OF ATTRACTION, SIMPLY PUT, IS THE ABILITY TO DRAW INTO our lives whatever we wish to be or have in our lives. So, if you are focusing on hate, you will attract hate. If you are focusing on happiness, you will find happiness. I want you to begin to focus on the things above instead of the things that are beneath you. Speak what you want to happen and watch what you plant with speech begin to manifest itself. Don't allow self-doubt to creep into your mind and cancel your future. Keep in mind, you are more than what others believe; you are special, and you have something to offer the world. I want you to speak life into yourself so much that you manifest your goals and others around you. If you want to know more about the law of attraction, please take some time to research some amazing concepts and beliefs on the law of attraction. Remember knowledge is an online search away.

Write what you want and how much you are worth.

Speak your dreams over and over throughout the day.

Take into account, the day you plant the seed is not the day you eat the fruit, so don't expect it to happen right away.

PART TWENTY-TWO

―――

Give to receive.

"Give and it shall be given to you: good measure, pressed down, shaken together and running over, will be poured into your bosom. For with the measure you use, it will be measured to you."

Luke 6:38 NKJV
Scripture taken from the New King James Version

I CAN TELL YOU FROM EXPERIENCE THAT THE ACT OF GIVING FEELS good. Giving your time to others takes your mind off of your own situation and focuses it on someone else. Giving opens the door for receiving to the giver. Concentrating all energy and time on making your dreams and goals come true can feel selfish. One act of kindness may be the key to unlock the door you need open. Amazing advantages can be realized just by giving to others.

Here are a few reasons why giving is important:

- Giving helps the less fortunate.
- Giving makes a difference in others' lives.
- Giving helps you build relationships with the people around you.
- Giving makes you happy and feel good.
- Giving help you set a good example for others.

Consider this, you don't just have to give to the homeless, you can volunteer, perform random acts of kindness, or become a mentor. If you want to know more about giving, pick up the book **The Go Giver** *by Bob Burg and David Mann, which studies the power of giving.*

How frequently do you give?

Do you think giving opens the door to receiving? Why?

List three reasons why you believe giving is important

1.)

2.)

3.)

PART TWENTY-THREE

Stop looking back.

THE ROAD TO SUCCESS CAN BE OVERWHELMING AND LONELY. YOU may feel like no one understands what you're going through, or you may be unable to see the light at the end of the tunnel. Never give in to self-doubt, naysayers, fear, or lack of confidence; continue to keep pushing even when you feel defeated. Sometimes, we look back and see how easy and relaxed life might have been before we began to push to achieve our purpose. Don't look back to give up, look back to pull someone along with you.

Here are some things to remember when you are on the road to first seek, next know, and then plan for your future:

- You are not alone.

- Set small goals and accomplish them one at a time.

- Get rid of the naysayers and ask for help

- Read daily inspirations.

- Believe in yourself and what you have to offer

Recall why you want to go after your goals and think about that when hurdles get in your way or you experience a setback. Find people who will push you forward and not impede your progress. Sometimes we have to be silent about our dreams and allow God to reveal them. When we reveal plans, some people may pray against us. Sometime silence is truly golden when it comes to reaching your goals. As you recall and pinpoint your goals. Answer these questions as a guide to stay focused.

Why would you look back?

Do you find yourself telling people your goals every time you come up with one? Why?

PART TWENTY-FOUR

Create a story.

TWO WORDS THAT PASTOR JOEL OSTEEN SAID THAT CHANGE MY LIFE and my way of thinking. I'm sure they will spark your way of thinking as well. "I Am"! Pastor Joel Osteen discusses "I Am" in his book called, *The Power of I AM*. We must be careful about what we speak throughout the day because our words have power. We can open our mouths and speak life or we can open our mouths and speak death. Words will plant seeds that will grow roots. Remember it is hard to destroy roots once they've become rooted and our words have the same impact. Daily affirmations create a daily story that eventually becomes your life. You can check out the daily affirmations I use on my website www.jump2soar.com. We much watch what words we speak over ourselves and others.

Here are a few things you should speak daily:

- I am blessed and favored.
- I am the head and not the tail.
- I am healthy and happy.
- I am loved.
- I am a winner.

Write out three things you will say every day that will help change your life.

1.)

2.)

3.)

Create your own story about what you want to happen in your future and use the words "I am going to...". This is your life, and only you can live it.

PART TWENTY-FIVE

Share and teach.

I HOPE YOU FOUND MY BOOK ENCOURAGING AND INSPIRING. WHEN we find treasures it is important that we share them with others. I pray that this book unleashes the fuel you need to push for what you truly want. Thank you, in advance, for reading and sharing these practices with others. My reason for writing this book is to inspire, encourage, and motivate individuals who feel lost on the road to success. This book is not just a one-time practice, continue to pick up this book to gain something new that will help you on your road to fulfilling your purpose. Remember, first seek, next know, then plan. As I shared with you, it is important to learn and share:

What did you learn from this book?

What was your favorite part of the book? Share on Instagram and tag me in it.

What lesson will you teach someone who is thinking about going after a career?